The All About Company

www.theallaboutcompany.co.uk

First published in Great Britain 2015 by
The All About Company (Lincs) Ltd.

Text and Illustration
Copyright © 2015 The All About Company (Lincs) Ltd.

ISBN 978-0-9928866-1-5

A CIP catalogue record for this book is available
from the British Library.

Page layout and design by Dai Thomas MCSD.

Disclaimer
Every effort has been made to attribute the quotations in this collection
to the correct source. Should there be any omissions or errors in this
respect we apologise and shall be pleased to make the appropriate
acknowledgements in any future edition.

Rugby
Tackled
a mothers' translation

Written by
Rebecca Chatterton with Annabel Buik and Tara Shippey

Illustrated by
Kate Spurway

This book is dedicated to our boys.
Keep on playing the games you love.

Contents

Introduction

Rugby is as British as mud and drizzle, two of the regular ingredients needed to enjoy the sport. It demonstrates that we are a nation that know what to do with a ball and a muddy field.

Rugby is war-like, it's tribal and adrenaline fuelled. In our modern health and safety-obsessed society, its violent energy seems almost out of place. It's a sporting contest that brings tears to the eyes of men with cauliflower ears and extensive dental work. It's played at all ages, levels and abilities - from school team or local rugby club, to contests on the international stage. On rugby pitches around the country, players of variable shapes, sizes and fitness are happy to throw away all sense of self-preservation for the sake of the game.

As an uneducated spectator, braving a school touchline on a wet and windy November afternoon, it can be hard to see the attraction. For those who understand the sport it seems an exciting game, but for those watching a pre-adolescent child being thrown into the fray, exciting is *not* the word. Strangely, most children seem to emerge elated from matches, even after an hour spent dragging each other through the mud. Exhausted, definitely, but still smiling, if a little weakly, from behind their gum shields. A peppering of stud marks to the thigh, stamped fingers and the early tingle of a nosebleed, will only heighten their sense of pride in a battle nobly fought.

Introduction

As three mothers with nine boys between us, we can barely count the hours spent on the touchline. It was there that it occurred to us that understanding the game better would enable us to enjoy watching the game more. We have bravely swallowed the rulebook on your behalf, and we can assure you, it's a pretty meaty tome. After all our hard work, we didn't want to be the only ones with strong post-match opinions around the tea urn. We aim to clarify what's happening on the pitch, from the apparent chaos of a ruck or maul to why a scrum or line-out might happen and why the brave referee seems to blow the whistle so tirelessly.

Children learning to play rugby are taught simplified rules according to their age. The hope is that they will enjoy the running, passing and teamwork of the game before learning the more complicated elements and the physical nature of the sport. Before you know it, the child playing in front of you is a fully-grown, bloodied warrior.

Be warned, some fellow spectators can be very passionate in bellowing advice while striding up and down the touchline. They are often 'retired players' who haven't played the game since school. Although dedicated touchline pundits and dispensers of advice both to players and referee alike, they speak a rugby language that will only confuse you and shed no light on the rules of the game. After reading this translation, you can stand equal to the 'experts'. Perhaps it will even ignite a love of the game in you too.

What is Rugby?

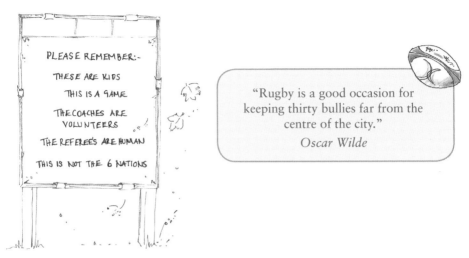

PLEASE REMEMBER:-

THESE ARE KIDS

THIS IS A GAME

THE COACHES ARE
VOLUNTEERS

THE REFEREE'S ARE HUMAN

THIS IS NOT THE 6 NATIONS

"Rugby is a good occasion for keeping thirty bullies far from the centre of the city."
Oscar Wilde

Rugby involves extreme physical contact between players. It brings to the surface instincts long supressed by public law and good manners. It's a game of evasion and possession where the object is to get hold of the ball and score points. It can't be played half-heartedly and the more fearless and pugnacious the players are, the greater their contribution is to their team - the muddier and bloodier - the better.

Rugby is a sport invented in an earlier, more brutal age, supposedly a product of the English public school system. Legend says that once upon a time (in 1823) there was a resourceful boy at Rugby School called William Webb Ellis. He became exasperated during a football match and decided to pick up the ball and run with it. So the modern game of Rugby football was created.

In reality, ball games that incorporated a mixture of running, passing and kicking had been played in villages all over Britain since before the Middle Ages. Huge teams of men and boys would maraud after a ball and batter each other in open battle. The version of the sport attributed to Webb Ellis looks rather genteel by comparison.

Rugby union is the form of rugby examined in this book. Although activity on the pitch can look like a violent free for all, there are in fact 22 laws which govern the game. These were first canonised in 1870 and have endless complicated subdivisions and clauses which have been revised over the years and are applied on the pitch by the referee and his trusty whistle. If you want to read the laws in full you can find them on the World Rugby website (www.worldrugby.org). Good luck!

> '**World Rugby**' is the international governing body of rugby union, the organisation was formerly known as the IRB (International Rugby Board).
>
> English rugby is governed by '**England Rugby**' formerly known as the RFU (Rugby Football Union).

The basics of the game

This book looks at the rules of rugby union as it's played from humble school pitch to international stadium.

The object of the game is for two teams of 15 players to get the ball over the opposition's try-line and down onto the ground to score a try. Team numbers are reduced for younger players (see page 91).

> The try-line and the goal-line are one and the same thing. We use both names throughout this book.

The 15 players are divided into the big heavies pushing from the front, known as the forwards, and a group of slightly smaller, quicker players who do more running and get the ball away. They are known as the backs.

The game is played on a rectangular grass pitch with a try/goal-line. A set of 'H' goal posts are positioned at each end.

The rules of rugby allow the egg-shaped ball (the technical word is elliptical) to be picked up, passed and kicked as it moves between players. When the ball is set down over the try-line points are scored and an accurate kick over the posts adds some more.

There are two main rules that give the game its character:
1. The ball can't be passed forward.
2. The player holding the ball can be grabbed anywhere below the shoulders and brought down by what is known as a tackle.

Learning to play

Young children start playing the game in the shape of tag rugby. This form of the game is a fun introduction to the basic passing, running and team skills needed. No tackling or contact is allowed. Instead players chase whoever has the ball and tear off tags worn around their waist (see page 89 for the rules of Tag rugby).

- **New rules of play**
  These have been introduced for children between the ages of 9 and 13. The aim is to bring more uniformity and inclusivity at youth level and so inspire a wider uptake of the game. Some schools have historically allowed teams of mixed age groups, but children will now need to play within their academic year. Many of the rules and particular skills needed for each specific position are introduced as children progress.

  By the age of 14 the rules of the adult game come into force (see page 91 for the new rules according to age).

The introduction of contact rugby can be a shock for some children (and their parents). Running with and passing the ball may have seemed fun, but the mental and physical commitment required to wrap your arms around someone's waist and push them aggressively until both of you tumble to the ground, can take time to learn. Some children choose never to get it... Rugby is *not* a game for everyone.

Women's rugby

Girls can play rugby in mixed teams until 12; often the flying ponytail is the only thing separating them from the boys. The women's game has grown quickly over recent years. Their teams are now an integral part of clubs and universities around the country, with an estimated 18,000 women and girls playing the game.

The Women's Rugby Football Union was formed in 1983 and the England women's team collects more trophies by the year. The female matches are played with exactly the same rules as those of their male counterparts.

Other formats of rugby

- **Rugby League** was formed shortly after Union. Its fan base is strongest in the north of England and the southern hemisphere. It has only 13 players to a team and the game takes place on a smaller pitch. After a tackle the ball isn't up for grabs but is kept by the tackled player who then gets to their feet and passes it on to a teammate. The side with the ball can be tackled 6 times after which the ball is handed over to the opposition if a try hasn't been scored. Unlike rugby union, there are no line-outs and no pushing in the scrum and forwards and backs are more physically similar.

"In south west Lancashire, babes do not toddle, they side-step. Queuing women talk of 'nipping round the blindside'. Rugby league provides our cultural adrenalin. It is a physical manifestation of our rules of life, comradeship, honest endeavour, and a staunch, often ponderous allegiance to fair play."

Colin Welland (1979)
Screenwriter of Chariots of Fire and a Lancastrian.

- **Rugby Sevens** is played on the same size pitch as rugby union but only has 7 players - 3 forwards and 4 backs. With more ground to cover and a shorter playing time of 7 minutes each way, the game is fast paced and requires the players to use speed, stamina and outstanding all round ball skills. Sevens is now an Olympic sport.

The Melrose Cup
The need to raise money for his Rugby club led Ned Haig to organise the first seven-a-side tournament in Melrose in the Scottish Borders in 1883. So the game of 'Sevens' was born and The Melrose Cup is still its most coveted prize to this day.

- **Touch Rugby** is a variation of tag rugby, played by older children and popular with adults. Gone are the ribbons used in tag but a tackle is made by a touch to the body below the waist. It keeps all the fun of the 15-a-side game without the messiness of tackling. There are no scrums or rucking and mauling. Like rugby league each side gets 6 touches of the ball before they have to hand it over to the opposition. The game is increasing in popularity and is a regular sight in parks and playing fields all over the country.

Nude Rugby
Giving a whole new meaning to the phrase 'flying tackle', Dunedin in New Zealand holds the annual Nude Rugby International. The host team, the Nude Blacks, take on invitational teams and all players compete in the buff.

International contests

Playing in international games and representing ones country earns a player their 'Cap', so called because competitors are given just that to mark the occasion.

- **The Rugby World Cup**
  Every 4 years, 20 of the world's greatest international teams battle it out for the William Webb Ellis Cup. The World Cup tournament sets the stage for legends to be born.

- **The Rugby Championship**
  The southern hemisphere's equivalent of the Six Nations is battled out between New Zealand, Australia, South Africa and Argentina.

> **The Kiwi Haka and psyching out the opposition**
> The ritual of the All Blacks performing the Maori Haka before international games has to be one of the most famous sights in rugby. This Ka mate, Ka mate chant was used traditionally to prepare warriors both mentally and physically and was first used before a rugby match in 1888. It works. The opposition try to look unfazed but the posturing of the Haka adds to the mystique and power of one of the greatest international sides in the world.

Nicknames of International Teams
The All Blacks - New Zealand
The Springboks - South Africa
The Wallabies - Australia
Les Bleus - France
The Pumas - Argentina

- **The British and Irish Lions**
Being made a Lion is something akin
to being canonised. This invitational
team chooses leading players from Great
Britain and Ireland to tour the southern
hemisphere every 4 years. Rugby pundits
have strong opinions on who should make
the cut and be pronounced the best of the
best. For many players being made a Lion
is a higher honour than being capped for
their country.

Domestic and European contests

- **The Premiership**
The annual English premier league championship is made
up of the 12 domestic rugby teams. Like any league, no
team can afford to be complacent as the bottom team each
year is relegated from the premiership.

- **The European Rugby Champions Cup**
This is the most prestigious cup to win in European club
rugby. The 20 qualifying spots in the tournament are picked
from England, Wales, Scotland, Ireland, France and Italy.

- **European Challenge Cup**
  The second tier of European rugby clubs play for this Cup, with clubs from lesser playing nations such as Romania.

- **The Six Nations**
  So that Rugby fans know it is spring, the Six Nations is a tournament held every year before Easter. England, Scotland, Ireland, Wales, France and Italy all play each other once and the tournament is won on points. As well as the main tournament itself, many other battles of honour are also fought. Should one team remain unbeaten they win the 'Grand Slam', England's clash with Scotland is played for the 'Calcutta Cup' and the winner from the home nations - England, Ireland, Scotland and Wales, takes the 'Triple Crown'.

The Barbarians
Fondly called the Baa-Baas, this invitational club was formed in 1890 and if there are any romantic ideas in rugby, this club takes the lot. Some of the worlds greatest players have joined its ranks, tasked not merely to win games, but to demonstrate rugby in its most elevated form.

The Rugby Pitch

> "Sticks and Stones may break my bones but rugby does it better."
>
> *Anon*

Rugby is usually played on grass, the muddier the better. Venues range from local recreational fields, school games pitches to club or league grounds. Players are adept at dipping themselves from head to toe in liquid Britannia, often barely able to move as their mud-caked limbs set by the end of the game.

Mud denotes soft ground - the friend and natural cushion to the falling rugger bugger. With safety in mind, schoolboy matches can be cancelled if the ground is considered too hard. Sadly, in the British rugby season this rarely occurs because of drought but more usually because of frost.

Hallowed stadiums

Twickenham, London - capacity 82,000
The home of English Rugby - need we say more?

Murrayfield, Edinburgh - capacity 67,800
The home of Scottish Rugby and the place Scotland really enjoys beating the "auld enemy", England.

The Millennium Stadium, Cardiff - capacity 74,500
The home of Welsh Rugby, built in 1999 to be the best rugby stadium in the world.

Aviva Stadium, Dublin - capacity 51,700
The home of Irish Rugby, rebuilt and opened in 2010 on the same site where games have been played since 1878.

The hallowed ground

Please use the diagram of the pitch to help make sense of our descriptions!

The area of the rugby field is marked out with white lines. Play takes place within the large rectangle created by the outer lines. This area measures up to 100 metres long by 70 metres wide and is then divided into 4 different zones, all marked with unbroken whites lines. The middle line is the halfway line, the lines on either side of it are called the 22 metre lines and at each end are the goal/try-lines with the distinctive 'H' goal posts standing in their middle.

- **The 22**

  This is the area in front of the goal/try-line which ends with the 22 metre line. It is a crucial part of the pitch where special rules can apply, but more of this later.

  The lines are marked with flags at the point where they intersect with the touch line. Being on the wrong side of a little bit of white paint can mean the difference between a try or no try, or the ball being given away to the opposition.

"In their 22".
Translated:
Any team who finds themselves defending inside their 22 metre line will be more than a little worried about the chance of their opponents scoring a try against them.

- **The in-goal area**

  This is the space behind the goal/try-line and the rugby posts. It finishes at the dead-ball line and is the important area where tries are scored. To score a try the ball must be put down anywhere in the in-goal area. Ideally it should be slammed down directly between the posts which makes the subsequent conversion kick (for extra points) a lot easier!

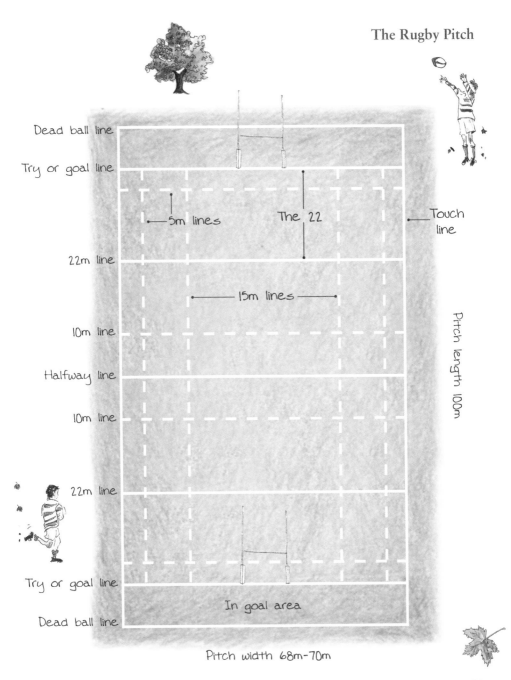

The Rugby Pitch

Dead ball line

Try or goal line

5m lines

The 22

Touch line

22m line

15m lines

10m line

Halfway line

10m line

22m line

Try or goal line

In goal area

Dead ball line

Pitch length 100m

Pitch width 68m-70m

- **The touchline**
  This is made up of 2 long lines which run the length of the rugby field. Inside the lines is the field of play and outside of these lines is known as in-touch, which is rugby speak for out. A ball can be kicked out or carried into touch by a player. When this happens the ball is automatically given to the other side.

- **The 5 and 10 metre lines**
  These are the broken lines. The 10 metre line is used to mark the distance drop-kicks need to travel at the start of the game. The 5 metre line marks the distance the ball must travel when thrown in at a line-out.

The posts

Standing at the centre of the goal-line, and impressive in size, are the 'H' goal posts unique to rugby. Full size goal posts have a distance of 5.6 metres between their uprights and their interconnecting crossbar is 3 metres up from the ground. Points are scored by kicking the ball between the uprights and over the crossbar. This can seem impossible to achieve when faced with some of the awkward angles from which some kicks must be taken. At these moments the posts loom large and the crowd is hushed, hopeful, until the touch judge raises his flag to signal success.

Rugby Commandment

5 points for a try when the ball is grounded over the opposition's goal-line.

2 points for a conversion when the ball is kicked over the bar after a try.

3 points for a successful kick at goal after being awarded a penalty.

3 points for a drop goal kicked when the ball is in open play.

The clubhouse

The clubhouse is very much at the heart of things. Near the pitch, it's the strange smelling building with changing rooms and grim toilet facilities. The two busiest areas on match days will be the kitchen hatch selling bacon butties and, of course, the battle-scarred bar.

On Sundays during the rugby season clubhouses are inclusive, family friendly places. However, after adult matches, they can transform into rowdy dens of legendary bad behaviour where warring teams put aside their differences (and injuries) to take up 'gentler' challenges such as 'boat races' or leading each other in bracing sing-alongs.

The Rugby Team

> "I can think of no other sport where the success of the team is shouldered so equally by everyone."
>
> *HRH Prince Harry, Opening Ceremony, Rugby World Cup 2015*

One glance at your average rugby side is enough to tell you that there's room for every shape, size and personality in the team. The only prerequisite is a basic lack of self-preservation. It's rather heart-warming to watch a group of such strangely mismatched individuals work together. Through a combination of brute force one minute and agility the next, they try to out-muscle and out-wit the opposition (depending on who has the ball) and score a try.

The days of communal bathing are long gone, but there aren't many sports where you share the blood, sweat and tears of your fellow players quite so literally.

When the team of 15 players emerge from the tunnel and onto the pitch at the beginning of a game, they probably look like some modern day cross between the Bash Street Kids and the sort of people you wouldn't want to bump into after dark.

In this chapter we explain the positions and roles of the players as they participate in the adult game. The variations for younger players, by age are explained on page 91.

The players' positions

So who are all these players and how do they work together? The founding fathers of Rugby, when they named positions on the field, had the wisdom to keep it simple. They knew that the participants on the pitch were keen to get down to battering each other and that, after repeated knocks to the head, jersey numbers needed to relate to a specific position. For example the hooker wears the number 2 jersey and the fly-half number 10.

> In Rugby you can ask someone what number they play just as easily as which position.

All players must be able to do the two things that rugby is best known for; passing the ball and tackling players on the opposite team. Every player is allowed to score a try. However you are less likely to see a forward lumber over the try-line and a back will never dirty his hands in the scrum.

Rugby Commandment
All players are expected to both defend and
attack, depending on whether they have the ball.
The team with the ball are attacking and the team
trying to get the ball back are defending.

The 15 players are split into two groups known as the forwards and the backs.

Think of the forwards as the heavies, the thugs and enforcers of this warring gang. There are 8 of them. Their role is to act as the battering ram that pushes the opposition back off the ball whilst attempting to gain possession.

The remaining 7 players are the backs. They form a line which fans out behind the forwards. When they get the ball they pass it along through their ranks using all the tricks of the trade, from dummy pass to sidestep, they, the 'wide men' get the ball away and dispose of it... hopefully over the try-line.

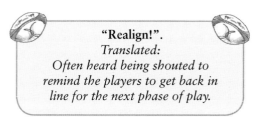

"Realign!".
Translated:
Often heard being shouted to remind the players to get back in line for the next phase of play.

The team

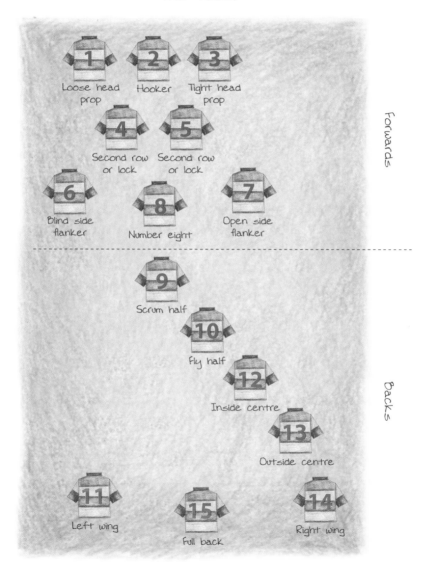

The forwards

Commonly known as the pack, the forwards can be separated into the 3 units that make up the lines they form in the scrum:

1. **The front row** - the loose head prop (no 1), the hooker (no 2) and the tight head prop (no 3) all at the gnarly end of the action.

2. **The second row** - the 2 locks (no 4 and 5) are the giants of the field.

3. **The back row** - the blindside flanker (no 6), the openside flanker (no 7) and the nameless number 8.

The front row and the second row are also described as the tight 5 or the front 5, snuggled together as they are with their arms locked around each other in an embrace that some would call hugging but in rugby is known as binding. This happens at key moments in the game such as in a scrum or maul.

The players on the back row of the scrum are known as the loose forwards. They get to extricate themselves from these aggressive bear hugs quickly to tackle the opposition and support the backs.

The scrum

Front row

Second row

Back row

• The front row

Props - the heavies

If your children or teenagers are strong, square and not easily intimidated, then this is the place for them. The props are the foundation of the scrum and some of the boldest and broadest bodies on the team- the bodyguards or immoveable heavies.

> In French rugby a prop has the noble name of a 'pilier' - a pillar.

In the scrum

- They are recognisable as the ones whose arms are interlocked under the hooker's shoulders as they 'prop' up the scrum and support the hooker. Their heads are pressed forward into the face of the opposing team. They need to be brave because nobody wants to be the one who blinks first. They have been taught how to ensure their side of the scrum doesn't collapse while driving the opposition scrum backwards. Keeping a scrum up requires coordinated strength and the referee watches carefully to ensure the safety of all involved.

The loosehead prop (no 1) is on the left hand side of the hooker. His position is easy to remember compared to the other prop since he has some breathing space with his head 'loose' on the left hand side of the scrum. This is the side where the scrum-half puts in the ball. He needs to support, balance and keep the scrum up whilst helping the hooker to get a clear view of the ball.

The tighthead prop (no 3) is positioned to the right hand side of the hooker at the heart of the scrum. His head is pressed into the opposition quite literally 'tight' between the heads of the facing hooker and the opposition's loosehead prop.

In the line-out
- The props typically lift the jumper to get to the ball.

The Dark Arts of the front row
Since it is difficult for the referee to see what's happening in the heart of the scrum it has traditionally been a place where nasty things go on. Physical warfare in the form of head boring, bristle scratching and ear biting are less common these days. Scrumcaps have reduced the tell-tale cauliflower ears a little. However, a sneaky front row player still has the means to distract the opposition with painful consequences.

The hooker - the psycho

The hooker is the squarest, shortest man on the field and always in the thick of things. He was certainly the toughest kid in the playground in junior school and a fearless scrapper who loves to goad the opposition.

In the scrum
- He's the psycho that the heavies are there to support. He places himself bravely at the heart of the action and it's therefore almost impossible for spectators to see what he's doing.

The props put their arms around him and hold onto his shorts and as the scrum meshes together he becomes suspended between them. The scrum-half puts the ball into the melée of bodies and the hooker uses his right foot to strike out. He hooks the ball back to the rest of his pack who continue pushing and rolling it back for the scrum-half to retrieve.

In the line-out
- The hooker is the one who throws the ball in. He calls to certain jumpers (in code) to let them know that the ball is for them.

Famous psycho hooker nicknames
The Pit Bull - Brian Moore, English hooker of the 90's
The Raging Potato - Keith Woods, Irish hooker of the 00's

• The second row

Locks - the enforcers

The locks are the second row of the scrum. Rugby pundits call them 'the engine room' of the team, but you can also think of them as the enforcers backing up the front row. They are often giants - so lofty that their heads exist in a whole different weather system. When they have the ball they are expected to punch holes in the oppositions' defence. In the olden days these punches could be literal. In rucks and mauls they shunt the opponents away.

In the scrum
- They are expected to use their legs to push and power the scrum forward. Positioned behind the hooker they reach up and between the legs of the props to create a sort of reverse wedgy while binding tightly to each other.

In the line-outs
- As if they weren't tall enough anyway, the locks jump up (with the help of the props) to reach incredible heights and pluck the ball out of the air before the opposition does. When they get the ball they either pass it away to the waiting scrum-half, or at least knock the ball so that it falls onto their side.

"Making some hard yards"
Translated:
The forwards have pushed on and made ground despite tough tackling from the opposition.

• The back row

The flankers - the wheeler-dealers

The flankers are the all-rounders of the pack, the wheeler-dealers, who are everywhere and provide a safe pair of hands. During broken play, which is when the ball is bouncing around unclaimed by either side, the persistent flankers are there to pick it up and steal it from their opponents.

They also work closely with the scrum-half, protecting him during scrummages (fancy rugby speak for a scrum).

The blind-side Flanker (no 6) stands on the narrow side closest to the touchline. He's often the larger of the flankers and knows how to use his bulk to stop any opposition players with the ball. His belt is probably notched with the most ferocious tackle count on the team.

The open-side flanker (no 7) is usually the quicker of the 2 flankers. He stands on the open-side of the scrum and has the best view of the ball when the opposition has won it. He's the intimidating thug who bears down on the ball carrier forcing him to pass it or be tackled.

> The 'open' side on a rugby pitch is the area of greatest distance between the ball and the furthest touchline.

In the scrum
- The flankers stand on each side of the scrum towards the back. They don't bind themselves on as tightly as the rest of the forwards and are ready to tear away after the ball or tackle the opposition's man, who will probably be a halfback.

A traditional nickname for the open-side flanker was 'the tearaway'.

In the line-out
- The flankers normally stand towards the back of the line-out.

Number eight - Mr Fixit

Uniquely the number 8 has no other descriptive addition to his name - he is just... "number 8". This could be because he is something of a Mr Fixit. A good no 8 needs to combine the physical strength and height of a forward with the agility and speed of a back. He's dexterous and athletic and is one of the links with the backline. As well as pushing and powering forward as part of the pack, he is alert to the movements of the scrum-half in case he needs to take control, pick up the ball and run with it as it comes out of the scrum.

In the scrum
- He's the final piece of the triangle at the back centre. He bravely binds on and puts his head between the 2 locks' bums. He's normally the last man to move the ball out with his feet before the scrum-half can pick it up and pass it out.

In the line-out
- Number 8 is usually positioned towards the back as a potential jumper.

The backs

While the forwards are busy happy slapping the opposition into surrendering the ball, the backs loiter waiting in a line to get their hands on the ball and score a try. It could be suggested that their shorts are slightly cleaner and their faces less battered.

All the backs must be able to catch high balls and be strong kickers. Like the forwards, the backs are split into groups:

1. **The half-backs** - the scrum-half (no 9) and the fly-half (no 10) who between them direct their teams' play and stand closest to the forwards acting as a link.

2. **The mid-field or three quarters** - the 2 centres (no 12 and 13) who attack and defend the middle of the field and the 2 wings (no 11 and 14) who wait for the ball to be sent out to them so they can run with it and score tries.

3. **The full-back** (no 15) - who hangs back and acts as the last line of defence or attacks with the other backs as needed.

• The half backs

The scrum-half - the terrier

The scrum-half is one of the smaller players on the pitch, quick, clever and never far from the ball. When the forwards get the ball he's always a step away ready to pass it on to the backs. A good scrum-half is expected to be instinctively strategic and able to read the game, spotting how and where it's best to attack and make ground.

At any scrum, ruck or maul the scrum-half triggers the rest of the backs to burst into action. He needs to be able to make long, accurate passes as well as picking up the ball from difficult angles and heights. He's often heard directing and berating his teammates.

At the scrum
- He puts the ball into the scrum and then acts as the link between the forwards and the backs by moving quickly around to the rear of the scrum to retrieve the ball. From here he can pass it out quickly and cleanly, kick the ball or he might even go for a glory run himself.

At the line-out
- He stands beside the line-out, ready to receive the ball when his team have won it.

Fly-half or outside half - the brains

The fly-half is the brains of the operation, the mastermind who waits for the brawn of the forwards to do all the hard work and for the scrum-half to get the ball out to him. He's the strategist who decides whether to run, pass or kick the ball and he's quick enough to avoid tackles. He calls the attacking moves for the backs and he needs to have excellent passing skills to whip the ball out into a space for the speedier outside backs. He will have a powerful and accurate boot since he's the one most likely to take the kicks.

• Midfield

Centres - the cool kids

The inside centre (no12) is a strong all-rounder who can play as a second fly-half. He has all the moves and passes and is always trying to make space for his fellow outside backs to run into. He should be a strong kicker and have a safe pair of hands.

The outside centre (no 13) is possibly the quicker of the two and able to run as quickly as any of the wings. He should be able to step on the gas, as it were, and duck and dive around defenders. If he can't avoid them, then he's brave enough to plough straight on through them. Both centres need to be strong tacklers and relish getting stuck in.

Left and right wing - the glory boys

If the centres are quick, then the wingers need to be quicker still - intent on the glory of a try. They wait for the ball to be passed out to them through the centres and dash through space with the fleetest of foot and a magnificent finish. They need to be able to kick the ball and chase it, as well as dropping back to catch high kicks from the opposition.

• The full-back

Full-back - the lone wolf

The full-back is the final member of the team. He lives by the mantra 'attack is the best form of defence' as he stands behind the line of the other backs. He is the last man to protect the try-line if the opposition  gets through. Legendary full-backs are also quick enough to race up into the line with the other backs and take a pass or be an extra man on the wing. As well as being brave and fearless tacklers, they are also needed to catch high balls kicked by the opposition and must be able to boot them back with interest.

Playing the Game

The lines on the rugby pitch can be easily explained, so too can the roles of each of the players but put players on the pitch ...add an opposing team, throw in a ball, blow the whistle for the start of the game and then see how confusing watching a match becomes!

The aim of the game is simple - to win. A team wants to get the ball towards the oppositions goal/try-line and touch it down thereby scoring a try. However, so many strange things happen along the way. Moments of free flowing running and passing are interrupted by flying tackles, bouts of wrestling and trampling and calls to form tortoise-shaped huddles of pushing and shoving bodies.

The ebb and flow of a match

Rugby games are played over 2 halves, each of 40 minutes at the highest level. Half time is 10 minutes and time is added on at the end for stoppages. Once the game begins action on the pitch is fast, frantic and exhausting for the players, and possibly the spectators too.

To help understand the objectives amongst all this ferocious energy on the pitch, let's imagine how a game might progress from kick-off through to the moment a try is scored. To keep track, let's call our teams the Whites and the Blues.

"Phases of play"
Translated:
Are the free flowing passages of play where the ball is passed around (otherwise known as open play). This happens between the breakdowns of the rucks and mauls when play is more static.

Kick-off

The contest begins, as in so many sports, with the toss of a coin between the 2 captains. The referee will ask the winning captain whether he wishes to kick-off first or pick an end. The captains' decision is affected by the wind direction, which he may want behind him, and any understanding he has of the way the opposition play.

Let's say the Whites' captain wins the toss and starts the game with a drop-kick from the centre of the halfway line. The ball has to travel forwards over the 10 metre line before hitting the ground. All the rest of the White team make sure they are standing behind the kicker and the opposing Blues must stand at least 10 metres ahead of where the kick is taken.

The chase is on.

> **Drop-kick**
> When the ball is dropped to the ground and then kicked as it bounces back up, or on the half volley.

Open play

Once kicked the ball will either hit the ground, bounce and be picked up, or it might be caught directly by a member of either team. In this case let's say the Blues have caught it and their player is suddenly the focus of everyone's attention. His teammates are ready to receive a pass and get the ball up the pitch past the Whites. Meanwhile the Whites are bearing down, determined to weigh in with a crunching tackle and stop the Blues' progress.

> Players can run wherever they want on the pitch BUT when they want to pass the ball to another teammate, they must not pass it forwards.

This free flowing part of the game where the ball is passed between players, is called open play.

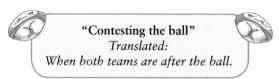

"Contesting the ball"
Translated:
When both teams are after the ball.

Moving the ball up towards the goal-line is a team effort. One lone ball carrier is easy prey so he shouldn't be isolated. The Blues should be running beside their player or finding spaces to run into so they can call for him to pass the ball.

So the Blue with the ball is running (this is his moment). It would make the game easier to explain if he could sprint off with the ball all the way to the try-line, but in reality several things could happen next.

1. Our player makes a mistake (what a shame).

The referee blows his whistle to stop the game for the following mistakes -

A forward pass
Guess what this is? This is the first potential slip-up a player under pressure might make. As he tries to get rid of the ball he could accidentally pass it to a teammate ahead of him. This forward pass halts the progress of the game and his team is penalised with a scrum to the other team (more of this in a minute).

A knock-on
As its name suggests, this is when the ball is not caught cleanly but dropped forward or comes off a players hand, arm, chest or head. Again, this halts the game and the team is penalised with a scrum awarded to the opposing side.

Any halt to the game caused by a forward pass or a knock-on, is called a stoppage. The game is started again which is called a restart. This is done with a scrum - the rules of which are explained on page 58.

"Playing the advantage"
Translated:
This is one of the trickiest rules to follow in rugby.
It happens when a referee decides to delay punishment for an offence and doesn't stop the game. He can decide to do this because the team who have got hold of the ball already have the advantage.

This rule was introduced to keep the game flowing.

---

2. Our player, in his efforts to avoid the opposition, sends the ball into touch.

Remember, the line on either side of the rugby pitch is called the touchline. When the ball goes over this line and hits the ground (or goes into touch) it is out. This could happen because a player:

- puts his foot on or over the line while running with the ball.

- is forced over the line by the opposition.

- kicks the ball ahead and out to make ground.

The result of this stoppage is a line-out, which we will explain on page 62.

"Crossing the line"
Translated:
If a player's foot touches the white line then he and the ball are considered out or in touch. BUT the ball can pass over the top of the touchline and not be out, if caught by a player mid-air and thrown back into play.

3. Our brave player is tackled before he can pass the ball to a teammate.

The moment a player is tackled and brought down, he should try to release the ball to a well placed team member.

"Offloading the ball"
Translated:
When a player gets rid of the ball to a passing teammate just before they are tackled.

Our player can be tackled in 2 ways:

a) if there is no one in the right place to pass to, he will run into the opposition and be brought down in a heap while still holding the ball. This is known as going to ground.

A player going to ground with the ball in his hands brings on the breakdown. This is when the ball is no longer in possession of one team or the other but up for grabs by both sides.

A ruck forms around the ball on the ground. It is hard to see what happens next and the murky details are explained on page 55.

b) the player with the ball is tackled and stopped but still on his feet. A wrestling contest, known as a maul, starts as the player wraps his arms around the ball to keep the opposition from ripping it out of his hands.

The intricacies of the maul are explained on page 53.

So how is our ball carrier caught out and brought down?

The tackle

If playing rugby is an expression of one's inner savage, then the tackle has to be its fiercest outburst. Tackling well is an art, carefully taught for maximum effect. In all usual social situations, one child leaping at another in order to bring them down would meet with the instant wrath of adults and general condemnation. Put this behaviour on a field with a rugby ball at stake however, and adult voices will be heard bellowing "Bring him down!!" or "Legs!!" from the touchline.

As children move from playing tag rugby to contact, the brave commitment needed to make a tackle will separate those who want to play the game from those who realise that this isn't for them.

• **Making a tackle**
Children are taught how to tackle and how to fall. This is, of course, so they can hit the ground safely. They also learn how to protect the ball when being tackled and place it in the best position for their teammates to pick up.

"Cheek to cheek, ring of steel, slide down"
Translated:
Young rugby acolytes might be heard muttering this under their breath when learning to tackle. The attacking player goes in low, his cheek towards the butt cheek of his target, he then encircles their waist tightly and puts the force of his weight into knocking or dragging his victim down.

49

• **Things to remember about a tackle:**

- Only the player carrying the ball can be tackled but they can be tackled by more than one person at the same time.

- It must be made below the shoulders. High tackles are dangerous and an instant penalty is awarded to the opposition.

- The player can fall down in a number of ways, from having one or both knees down, to sitting on the ground or in the most usual manner, lying face down in the mud.

- The player holding the ball must let go or release the ball as soon as he has gone to ground.

- The tackler must let go as soon as he has brought down the player, roll away from the ball and get to his feet before trying to grab the ball.

The Hit
This is the impact of a tackle, the moment that two competing forms of muscle and brawn or perhaps moobie and paunch come together as one player tackles another.

• **A missed tackle**
This is when the hunted player gets away. Every young player dreams of pulling off a cunning sidestep or a display of sheer power and pace to push on through, shaking off the tackles in his wake.

The turnover

So, back to the game, Whites versus Blues. Our Blues player has been successfully tackled and is on the ground. The ball is now being fought over by both sides or in other words contested. If someone from the White team manages to pick up the ball and pass it on, then this is known as a turnover. One side had the ball but has lost it.

Scoring a try

The Whites have won the ball. If this part of the game takes place behind their own 22 metre line they must be on high alert as this area is directly in front of their own try-line, which is the line the oppostion want to cross to score against them.

The Whites need to get the ball back up the field as quickly as possible, but under pressure one of them makes a duff pass. Suddenly the ball is back with the Blues. Several quick passes later and despite the Whites' efforts, the Blues carry the ball successfully over the Whites' try-line to be put down firmly in the in-goal area. Another diving hero added to the Blues' hall of fame.

They have scored a Try! Score: 5 points

> The ball must be grounded with downward pressure on or over the try/goal-line and in the in-goal area for a try to be allowed.

Conversion

The Blues' spectators celebrate. Then a hush falls on the crowd in anticipation of the conversion kick. The player with the strongest and most accurate boot, places the ball back on the ground in line with the spot where the try was scored.

Goal kicks are often taken from very difficult angles. This is because the kick must be made in a line with the point where the ball was touched down. If this is either to the very far left or right of the posts the kicker is allowed to move as far back up the pitch as he thinks his kick can travel to open up the angle. This is why players scoring a try aim to put the ball down as close to the posts as possible.

It seems all the rage for kickers these days to have special ways of measuring their run up or to adopt prayer-like stances before sending the ball sailing over the cross bar and between the posts.

The perspective of the ball versus the posts can play tricks on the eye. The touch judge's raised flag is often the only way to be sure a kick has gone over successfully.

Conversion! Score: 2 points

> **The kicking tee**
> A circular piece of plastic used to hold the ball up and steady on the ground from where conversions and penalty kicks are taken.

Inside a Maul and Ruck

We have looked at when a tackle is made as part of the general flow of a rugby match. The tackle is the moment when rugby moves from being a game of evasion to one of contact - although contact is a wonderful understatement for the thumping power of a successful tackle.

A ruck and maul are the result of a tackle and this phase of the game is called the breakdown.

The breakdown

Suddenly the ball and the man who was tackled are at the centre of a frenzied mess of bodies. The maul and ruck might look the same to the untrained eye but there is a key difference - a maul takes place when the ball carrier at the centre of it is still on his feet and a ruck takes place when the ball carrier has been properly tackled and pulled down to the ground.

Let's see inside the giant bear hugs and be enlightened.

The maul

A maul happens when the man with the ball is tackled but through sheer strength manages to remain standing.
The man tackling him holds him up in a bear hug on one side, whilst trying to reach round and get the ball. The ball carrier's team will immediately come to support on the other side and help him by binding onto him from the back. (Remember, binding is what players do when they hold onto each other.)

• **The rules of a maul**

It's no coincidence that bears maul their prey:

- Players joining a maul have to be careful that they aren't offside. They must come in from behind the hindmost foot of the last teammate. Coming in from the side will be penalised by the referee.

- Players in the maul must have their heads or shoulders no lower than their hips and have at least one arm bound to a teammate.

- For safety reasons, the team who don't have the ball can be penalised for either deliberately collapsing the maul or for attempting to drag players out of it.

- To get the ball out of the maul players must pass it backwards until it eventually reaches a man who has the space to get it away.

"Recycle the ball"
Translated:
When a team goes into a maul or ruck with the ball and emerges with it still in their possession.

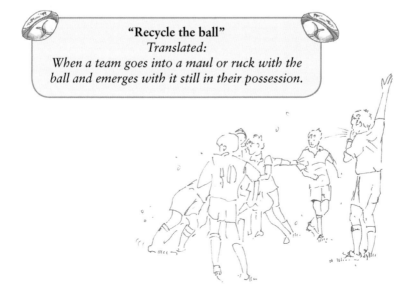

• **A rolling or travelling maul**

This looks like something straight out of a medieval battle plan and is every bit as effective as a form of attack. Players, especially the forwards, love this way of gaining ground against the other side by shoving and driving forwards to create a human battering ram against the other team. While this is happening the ball will have been passed back further into the mass of bodies for protection. Excitement grows as momentum builds and if the maul is close to the other team's try-line they have the chance to push the maul over the line and plant the ball down to score a try.

"Use it or lose it"
Translated:
The referee will decide to penalise the team taking the ball into the maul if they don't keep momentum going forward or pass the ball back, by awarding a scrum to the other side.

The ruck

A ruck is what happens when the man with the ball is brought down to earth with a tackle.

If he hasn't managed to pass or offload the ball before he hits the ground, his teammates move in to create a protective cage over the top of him. The centre of the ruck can be a nasty place. Once the vulnerable player has let go of the ball and put it in a spot accessible to his team, it is usual to see him lying curled up with his hands over his head. Mothers - try not to panic, instead yell "Ruck over!"

• **The rules of the ruck**

- The player who made the tackle must roll away and neither he nor any of his teammates are allowed to pick up the ball if they have one or both knees on the ground. (That's not to say they don't make a sneaky attempt to do so if they think the ref can't see.)

- The player holding the ball must let go of it, so he places it in a spot easily accessible to his teammates. This action is grandly referred to as presenting the ball and ignores the chaos happening all around.

- Players who join the ruck must do so behind the hindmost foot of the last player.

- Teammates of the tackled player are allowed to pick the ball up with their hands as long as they are still on their feet and aren't part of the ruck. However, as the number of players joining the ruck rises so it becomes harder to reach in and get to the ball. This is where the game of footsie starts and the ball is usually inched out by deft footwork. This is what the word rucking actually means. Referees are strict in ensuring that players don't deliberately stamp on each other but it isn't always easy to distinguish a dirty trick from an accident.

'**Through the gate**'
Translated:
This is the only way to enter a
maul or ruck, i.e. from the back.

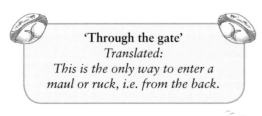

The Scrum and the Line-out

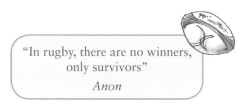

"In rugby, there are no winners,
only survivors"
Anon

The scrum and the line-out are those chaotic-looking episodes
you will see happening time and again on the pitch. Contrary
to received opinion, they are neither giant scraps for the ball
nor exaggerated pogo-ing competitions. They are called set
pieces (a title more suited to ballroom dancing, perhaps) and
are used to restart the game after minor infringements or
when the ball has gone into touch.

The scrum

When a player makes a mistake such as knocking the ball on,
passing it forward or putting himself offside, rugby considers
this a minor infringement that requires a stoppage of the
game. The game is restarted with a scrum. The opposing
team is given the ball to put into the scrum and so gain the
advantage, but more of this in a minute.

The scrum is one of the most iconic sights in a game of rugby
and also one of the most controversial. In recent years new
rules have been introduced to stop scrums collapsing and
to prevent the injuries that this can entail. The new rules
put more emphasis on the way the two sides bind together
rather than the powerful butting against each other, known
as engaging. This is when the forwards of both teams lock
together, head to head, to form a dome of bodies.

• **Forming a scrum**

All the forwards from each side are involved in the scrum. Players fit together like a human jigsaw puzzle with each side intending to out-muscle the other.

To form a scrum, the referee gives the instruction to both packs to "crouch, bind, set". Traditionally this locking of horns had the weight and impact of a head-on train collision. The professional forward of today's pack has more muscle per inch of body fat than ever before. The new laws of the scrum hope to manage this.

"The hit"
Translated:
The full power of impact as both packs come together (imagine one of those nature programmes where the two giant walrus males bash into each other).

• **The rules of the scrum**

- Props aren't allowed to grip their opponent's chest, arm, sleeve or collar (please read instead - nipple, ear or beard).

- When "crouch, bind" is called, the props use their outside arm to grip their opposite number.

- There will be a strained pause while they balance, then the referee will shout "set" and the opposing front rows engage (please read - power into each other with grunts and bellows).

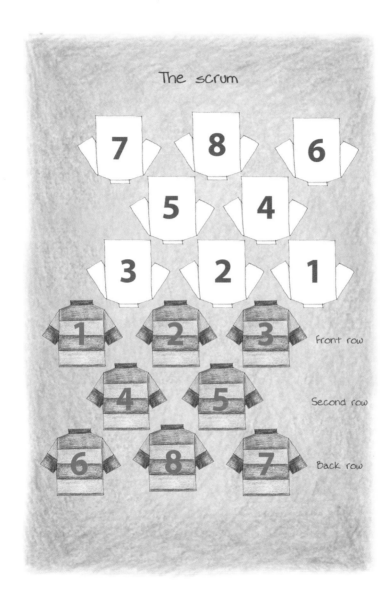

The scrum

Front row
Second row
Back row

With everyone straining away in a balanced scrum, the referee signals he is happy and the scrum-half with the ball will put it into the tunnel created by the two packs (in a straight line). The two hookers then play footsie for the ball. Hopefully the team who had the put-in will manage to hook the ball back towards their half of the scrum.

While this is going on the two packs are constantly shoving against each other and trying to push the other side back and make ground.

"Wheeling the scrum"
Translated:
A devious and illegal tactic employed by the forwards to push the opposing team off the ball by turning the scrum 'accidentally'.

The scrum-half moves around to stand at the rear of the triangle of his pack where he expects the ball to emerge from under the feet of the players. He peers into the dark tangle of feet seeking out the ball before doubling over to scoop it from the ground and pass it on, usually to the fly-half.

The Line-out

The line-out is used to restart the game when the ball goes out into touch. Of course, simply handing the ball over to be thrown back onto the field (as football does) would remove the element of physical contest. To this end, the line-out is formed.

To bestow the advantage to the non-offending team, their hooker is given the ball and he stands just behind the touchline at the point where the ball went out. The team with the ball decides how many players will make up the numbers in the line-out. The forwards of both teams form two lines in front of the hooker, side by side, a metre apart and at right angles to the touchline. The hooker, probably half the height of the men in front of him, throws the ball in through this avenue of giants with the expectation that his team can get their hands on it.

To help them with this most teams develop simple but possibly silly codes which are shouted by the hooker or pack leader. Schoolboy line-out language and calls can be very creative! There is nothing in the rules to say that the ball must be thrown and not rolled. Teams should beware the smaller boy standing at the front of the line-out seemingly tying his shoelaces, only for the ball to be thrown towards him by his hooker. No lifting is allowed in the line-out until the Under 16s age group.

At club and international levels spectators are treated to the sight of the human skyscrapers in the line-out being supported by their teammates to reach ridiculous heights in order to snatch the ball. Extra gripping power is given by bandages and strapping that adorn the thighs of some of the pack. (This could of course also be part of the patch up efforts of the physio to protect previous injuries.)

• **The rules of the line-out**
Such fierce competition ensures that the line-out is a set piece where the ball can be won by either side, regardless of who throws it in:

- The ball must travel 5 metres into the line-out.

- A player can't be tackled whilst in the air.

- Argy bargy such as shoving will be penalised with a penalty kick awarded to the non-offending side.

- Any player who is off the ground and supported by their teammates must be held onto until they reach the ground. In other words a player can't be dropped just because they fail to get the ball.

- The player who catches the ball either passes it on to another player (most likely the scrum-half) or keeps hold of the ball and starts a maul. So the game moves on.

• A quick throw-in

A quick throw-in can be taken before a line-out forms. The ball must have gone into touch and been caught over the line by a player from the non-offending side. If he sees one of his teammates nearby he can throw the ball in quickly, as long as he himself stays in touch. Simple really.

> A note of warning to any enthusiastic touchline spectators - a quick throw-in will not be allowed if the ball is picked up and handed to the player by a 'helpful' bystander.

"Awarded a Penalty"
Translated:
The referee does this a lot. If a side is awarded a penalty it is a good thing. It can be confusing to those new to rugby because it sounds negative. The referee awards a penalty to the non-offending side who are then given the ball to either run with or kick.

Free kick
Awarded for minor infringements.
It can be used to:
- kick to touch
- form a scrum
- tap the ball and run

The Referee

> "Players and spectators at all levels can enjoy the sport so much better if they totally accept two simple rules.
> Rule one: the referee is always right.
> Rule two: in the event of the referee being obviously wrong, rule one applies"
>
> *Peter Corrigan, sports journalist*

The referee is a brave, fit man.

He can sometimes cut a lonesome figure, running around on the pitch amongst 30 aggressive players, socks pulled up neatly over his shapely calves. He's there to act as the 'sole judge of fact and law' (according to World Rugbys' rules.) He knows that Right is on his side, as is his whistle, which he clutches for comfort and blows on enthusiastically. Little armour, but this is enough. Rugby players the size of mountains switch immediately from blood crazed savages to meek compliant children when reprimanded by the ref. Only the captain of each team will dare to reason with him over a suspect decision.

"Killing the ball"
Translated:
When a player lies over the ball to stop the opposition getting at it. This is very naughty and a penalty is given to the other side.

The Referee

At the beginning of the match the referee brings the captains together to toss a coin and determine who will kick-off. He upholds law and order during the game and keeps time through out the match. He has the discretion to add on extra minutes for any stoppages due to injury, substitution or disciplinary issues. In the fray, the referee blows his whistle so frequently that he seems in danger of swallowing it (and there are many players who wish he would just go ahead and do so.) He's marking the beginning and end of each half, stopping play during the match or indicating that points have been scored.

The referee needs to be close by the action at all times but not in the way of the players or the ball. He has to see through the steam and into the scrum, or past the limbs and into the darker regions of a ruck or maul. He has to try and spot every 'accidental' stamp, slight of hand or harmful infringement. His decision is final.

At junior level, being arbiter of the game can be a thankless task. As well as understanding the minutae of the varying age rules, the referee has to apply a certain amount of discretion to keep the game moving and the children learning... and warm. In these circumstances, it is often the spectating parents who need to try and abide by his decisions. Referees sometimes have to suffer the advice of 15+ pairs of possibly biaised eyes replaying his every decision.

The advantage rule

Of the many World Rugby laws the referee must enforce - the advantage law can be the most contentious. It takes precedence over most other rules in the game and was developed to keep play going despite minor infringements. It can prove especially useful as children are learning the game. Playing the advantage happens when a referee decides to delay punishment for an offence and doesn't want to stop the game. He can decide to do this because the team who would benefit from the penalty have the ball anyway and so have the advantage already!

The television match official

In international and premiership games the referee is wired, literally, and it is usual to see him place his hand to his ear piece as he asks for a second opinion from the somewhat controversial Television Match Official or TMO. This camera based referee can view the game from angles not open to his counterpart on the ground. In the old days the referees judgement and subsequent decision was final, now some would suggest it is being undermined by technology.

The touch judges

The referee's only support down on the pitch are the 2 touch judges. They are the people jogging up and down on the touchline on either side of the field. Their key prop is their flag which they raise above their heads to signal the point at which the ball leaves the main playing area and goes over the line into touch.

When there is a kick at goal, the touch judges stand behind the goal posts and raise their flags to signal that the ball has gone over and for the crowd to roar accordingly.

Arm signals

Exaggerated arm gestures accompany the referee's whistle. These gesticulations aren't the first signs of a man losing the plot but are the signals that law and order is being enforced amongst the testosterone fuelled commotion.

A try has been scored or a penalty try has been awarded (the referee runs under the post and holds his arm up for a penalty try).

A penalty kick.

A knock-on.

A free kick.

A forward pass or knock-on.

An advantage is being played.

A scrum is awarded.

Foul play and infringements

> Foul play or an infringement is defined in rugby law no 10 as "anything a player does within the playing enclosure that is against the letter and spirit of the Laws of the Game. It includes obstruction, unfair play, repeated infringements, dangerous play and misconduct which is prejudicial to the Game"

No dangerous tackling, kicking, punching or stamping when the referee is looking. The list of potential fouls is limited only by imaginations dulled by repeated knocks to the head.

• A yellow card
If foul play does occur or the referee has had words with the culprit before, he can decide it is time for a yellow card. Any player who finds this waved in his face is sent off the pitch for a 10-minute sulk.

> **The Sin Bin**
> A shameful place to be. Players who are sent off to sit on the bench for 10 minutes because of a yellow card are letting themselves and their side down. Their team are left vulnerable with only 14 men on the pitch.

• A red card
The referee's final sanction, it is rarely seen in the game and means a permanent exit from the pitch for the offending player.

The Technical Stuff

Aside from all the grabbing and wrestling, or should we say the scrummaging, tackling and contact side of matches, rugby is a running and passing game. Referred to as open play this is the part of the game where the ball is moved quickly between the players.

When these players with the ball get going, they really get going. This is the exciting sort of rugby that fans want to see - where the pace of running, especially by the backs, is breathtaking and the technique shown in their passing is often inspirational.

Carrying the ball

As children begin to play the game, they are taught to hold the ball in two hands; only later in their playing career will they dare to tuck it under one arm while using their other hand to push away any oncomers attempting to tackle them. Dropping the ball and giving the opposition the chance to pick it up is something that no player ever wants to do.

"Strong with the ball in hand"
Translated:
Every player hopes to be described in such a way (especially the forwards). It means keeping their hands on the ball at all costs particularly in a ruck or maul where it could be ripped from them. It also means that they pass cleanly to their teammates.

Running

The backs do the majority of the running. Like one half of a red arrows display, they start in a fanned-out line, tracking the person ahead with the ball. They quickly move out from this formation to wherever they are needed - rugby players are always looking for space to run into. Should some beefy defender from the other team have them in their sights, then players are taught to run towards the inside shoulder of this defender creating more space for a teammate running in to take their pass.

Decoy running is a clever little trick up every players sleeve. As its name suggests it's a run used to confuse the opposition and draw them away from the player who's really about to catch the ball.

"Find space!"
Translated:
Something coaches are heard yelling at young
players. One of the key skills in rugby is to find
a gap to run into and hopefully catch and carry
the ball forward. This can be a pretty tricky
thing to do amongst all the rumpus on the pitch.

Passing

Players want to pass the ball to teammates who are in a better position. Ironically the game demands they pass the ball backwards to move it forwards up the pitch. They also pass when they are about to be tackled and lose the ball, this is known as off-loading.

• **Types of passes**

Players learn to pass the ball at chest height and different circumstances require different passes:

Long pass - need we explain?

Scrum-half pass - this is a pass which is used as the link between the forwards and the backs, though it can be used by any player to pass the ball away from a ruck or maul. It's a pass from the ground, which is swept up either to the left or right.

Spin pass - often used by the scrum-half, the ball is spun to make it travel further and faster. It's a good pass for long distances.

Scissors pass - a slick and effective pass when well drilled. The player with the ball draws any defence along with him and then just before he's tackled he turns towards the teammate tracking behind him to pass the ball. This teammate can then run on with the ball passing behind the tackled player and the opposition, making a cross like open scissors!

Dive pass - when a player isn't quite in position he dives forward and throws the ball at the same time.

Pop pass - a short looped pass that seems to hang in the air waiting for the recipient to dash through at speed and pick it up.

Flick and reverse flick pass - a short pass sent on its way with a flick of the wrist.

Overhead or lob pass - used by players to get the ball over the head of the opposition and into a space on the pitch.

One handed pass - usually made by a man under pressure because he's using his other hand to shove an attacker away!

> **"A hospital pass"**
> *Translated:*
> *Pity the poor player who happens to receive this*
> *- the worst kind of pass made to someone in a*
> *position so bad that they are certain to be tackled*
> *and taken down as soon as the ball reaches them!*

- **The Dummy**

There are also clever ways *not* to pass the ball:

Dummy pass - 'selling a dummy' is a swish move that all players want to perfect. The attacking player with the ball fools the defender into believing he's about to pass, only to keep hold of the ball and sprint away at the last moment.

Dummy scissors pass - (as before) the pass is called but not carried out, thus foxing the opposition!

Dummy kick - yes, you guessed it - the player pretends they are about to kick the ball but passes it instead.

All these sneaky moves go to prove how eagle-eyed a player needs to be and that the compliments of being able to "read the game" or having "good hands" are high praise indeed.

Catching

As we have just seen, the ball can be passed with such sleight of hand that rugby players need to be able to catch a ball from any height or angle. It can come from anywhere; a pass from a teammate, a ball intercepted from the oppostition or a high kick gathered in. To make matters more interesting the shape of the ball allows it to be spun for speed and power. Then there's the unpredictable nature of its bounce. Players need to catch the ball in the air to control it. Brave is the player facing down a ball booted from the other end of a rain sodden pitch.

Kicking

Rugby is primarily a running and passing game but it's also about gaining territory. One of the quickest ways to do this is to give the ball a jolly good boot. Not forgeting that a goal kick is another way to gain points.

> All good kickers factor in the wind. It can act as friend or foe depending on its direction!
> The sight of the focused kicker picking up some grass and letting it float to the ground is a familiar one.

• Kicking for touch

Kicking for touch is a phrase you will hear commentators use time and again during a game. This is when players deliberately kick the ball into touch, i.e. over the touch-line, off the pitch and out of play.

• **Rules for kicking into touch**

- Players kick the ball into touch to gain ground and get the ball away.

Kicking from outside the 22 - the ball must bounce before it goes into touch. At this point there is a line-out or quick throw-in given to the opposition at the place where it went out. Ground is gained for the kicking team even though the ball is passed to the opposition.

If the ball doesn't bounce before it goes into touch, the line-out or quick throw-in is taken back to the point from where it was kicked. No ground is gained for the kicking team and the advantage passes to the opposition who are given the ball.

Kicking from inside the 22 - a different rule applies. The kicked ball is allowed to go directly into touch and the line-out or quick throw-in is taken at this point and not sent back to square one. The kicking team, who were under threat in their own 22, are no longer at risk of the opposition scoring a try although, they will lose possession of the ball.

"Mark!"
Translated:
A player may signal this when he has caught a high ball in his own 22 metre zone.
All other players must back off and if he manages to take the catch cleanly he can then punt the ball back up the pitch.

• **Different kicks**

The shape of the ball means it can move in different ways in the air. Straight kicks out of the hand are known as punts and punts that spiral are called screwballs or spiral kicks:

Drop-kick - used to start the game or to score 3 points via a drop goal, the ball is dropped from the hands and kicked as it rebounds back from the ground.

"Charging down a kick"
Translated:
This is when a brave player from the opposition puts their body in the way of a kick. An intimidating move and any bounce off their body by the ball is not considered a knock-on and so play can continue.

Punt - sometimes known as kicking from the hand - this is used to send the ball out, into touch or as a clearance kick.

Place kick - used to score a conversion after a try has been made. Kickers use a kicking tee to balance the ball. Also used to kick a penalty.

Box kick - used in tight attacking or defensive situations, such as behind a ruck. The player wants to gain ground by kicking the ball high in the air and a little way ahead (into an imaginary box). This gains time for the player either to follow the ball and catch it or for one of their team to get underneath it, catch it and elude defenders.

> ### The 22 metre drop-out
> This happens when the attacking team punt the ball upfield and it crosses over the defenders goal/try line. This is a godsend for the defending team who, after touching the ball down quickly, can restart play with a drop kick from their 22 metre line.

Cross kick - a diagonal kick across the pitch to get the ball beyond any defender.

Chip and chase - a short shallow ball intended to loop over any headlong rush of the oppositions defence.

Grubber - a low bouncing kick along the ground making the ball awkward to pick up.

Up and under kick - also named the 'Garryowen' after the Irish team that perfected this kick. The ball is kicked high and far into opposition territory. As is to be expected given its place of origin, this kick is particularly effective on filthy wet days where it puts some hapless full-back under particular pressure, both to catch the slippery ball and to face down the ugly mob following it.

> "A kick is only as good as a chase"
> *Translated:*
> *It is all very well kicking the ball away from trouble but a player needs his determined teammates to be there to pick it up.*

The Rugger Bugger

Those Sunday mornings spent squeezing cold little
feet into rigid, mud-caked boots pass all too quickly.
Before you know it, a fully-fledged rugger bugger has
grown before your eyes.

• Matches

The rugger bugger comes alive on match days,
especially during international clashes. The television
is commandeered or better still, tickets are snapped up
months in advance. Rugby matches are boisterous and
boozy but usually quite harmless events. Take children to
watch a game at Twickenham, England's most hallowed
rugby ground, and you are unlikely to hear anything more
offensive than a plummy accent. Alcohol-fuelled incidents
tend to be limited to spilled pints as your neighbour jumps
for joy when a try is scored.

Alcohol is still sold at rugby matches and consumed in
vast quantities by spectators in their seats. This is the best
indication, if any was needed, of the good-natured, if
somewhat rowdy character of the crowd.

• Singing

When rugger buggers sing on the terraces it tends to be
clean and patriotic (they save the X-rated stuff for later
on in the bar.) National anthems such as "Flower of
Scotland", the beauty of a Welsh male voice choir singing
"Bread of Heaven" and the complicated French tune of
the "Marseillaise" are belted out as tears prick the eyes
of players and spectators alike. Shirts are clutched and
chests are thumped during these anthems - all an integral
part of the important process of psyching up for battle. In
recent years the English have adopted "Swing low, sweet
chariot, comin' for to carry me home" as their terrace chant,
blissfully unaware of the majority of the lyrics.

• **The rugby tour**
Rugger buggers love to go on tour. They commission special
tour tops and make their way to another part of the country
or world, on the hunt for fresh blood to play. Watching the
tourists jog onto the field is a fascinating study in the diversity
of the human physique, whether it be honed in the gym or
the pub. By day the team batter their opponents on the pitch,
and by night continue the assault socially. Rugby tourists
are infamously skilled at inflicting more harm on themselves
than anyone else, although the occasional road cone can get
into trouble. The phrase "what goes on tour, stays on tour"
applies here and it's difficult to extract many of the gruesome
details. Rumour has it that key tour ingredients include the
giving of silly nicknames, some form of badly timed group
nudity, x-rated sing-alongs, and the drinking of unspeakably
vile cocktails.

Inside the Kit Bag

Your average rugby player doesn't carry much kit.
In fact, at the beginning of any childs' career in the
sport, a parent can get away with buying some boots
and a special little bag to carry them in (bearing the
emblem of their local team). If you're lucky, it will
just be roomy enough to squeeze their gumshield in
too once they start playing contact.

It says much about the mentality of the sport that those who
enjoy this most physically abrasive game have historically
armed themselves with nothing more than strapping tape.
Want to protect those ears? Swathe them in tape. Dodgy
knee? Strap it up with tape. Need a lift in the line-out? Lash
those thighs with gripper tape. For this reason Rugby has
always snorted in derision at any suggested similarities with
its Amercian Football counterpart. Rugby's pared down ethos
of man with ball couldn't be more at odds with those over
padded, helmet-toting, Yankee wimps.

Times are changing though. The young generation of rugby
players isn't immune to the allure of a neon coloured boot
or the caress of carbonyte base layers, otherwise known as
skins, against their flesh. Every parent welcomes the general
acceptance of the scrum cap, gumshield and in some cases,
body armour.

The ball

The rugby ball is the perfect shape to be flung around the pitch by both throwing and kicking. Eliptical, or egg-shaped, it's made up of four panels stitched together and in adult size roughly 280-300mm in length. Although its design has changed little since the 19th century, the leather of the balls has been replaced by synthetic materials.

Why are rugby balls egg-shaped?
The first rugby balls were made by wrapping an inflated pig's bladder in leather, hence their elongated shape. An enterprising cobbler from Rugby called William Gilbert started supplying them to the school. The name 'Gilbert' is still recognisable on modern rugby balls today. Luckily, technology has moved on and the ball no longer shares its inners with a pig.

 Balls come in different sizes for the ages playing.

Ball size	Age group
3	Under 9
4	9-14/15
5	14/15+

Boots

Boots come in an array of colours to suit every dandy's taste and ensure a flash of theatricality during try-line dashes. When buying them, remember to take thick rugby socks!

Traditionally rugby boots have screw-in studs on the underneath of their soles and come with a little spanner for loosening and tightening. Regulations state that studs mustn't be any longer than 21mm which is practically high heeled. Lost or worn studs can be replaced easily and the life of the boot extended.

There are two types of stud pattern on boots: the 8 stud or the 6 stud. The 8 stud is most often worn by the tight forwards (props, hooker and locks) and gives extra grip for scrummaging and mauling. The 6 stud is worn by the backs for greater agility and quicker movement.

As the gap between the design of football and rugby boots narrows, many parents choose to buy their children football boots and put rugby studs on them in the rugby season.

One of the greatest enemies of the rugby boot is mud itself. Dried mud left in the stitching and caked onto the laces quickly rots and ruins a pair of boots, although we all know that the last thing on anyones mind when huddled back at home in the warmth, is cleaning them.

Protection

• Gumshields

Wearing a gumshield on the rugby pitch is compulsory, thank goodness. Designed to protect a player's smile, these rubber-like and often garishly coloured mouthguards give that uniquely menacing quality to grins from the field.

Custom-fit or boil and bite is the question. Once contact starts many schools bring in outside organisations to fit custom-made gumshields, OPRO being the best known. Boil and bite mouthguards prove useful for younger children and teens under the thrall of the orthodontist. They are designed to mould after being dunked in boiling water and can be reshaped as needed. It's a good idea to keep some boil and bite gumshields handy for when the grimy, unhygienic original inevitably gets lost.

• **Scrumcaps**

Scrumcaps are a common sight on the pitch these days, from youth rugby up to international levels. It's hard to believe they were controversial when first introduced and that some hard nuts of the scrum would never be seen wearing such a 'sissy' thing. Worn to protect the head from scrapes and bumps, scrumcaps also lesson the damage to the ear cartilage and minimise the Frankenstein's monster look so prevalent in forwards of previous generations.

In modern rugby, scrumcaps are seen on players in all positions across the team. They don't prevent concussion but are better than nothing. At junior level they can certainly help the emotional state of any parent who watches their child curled up amongst the trampling boots at the bottom of a ruck.

Cauliflower ears
The wearing of these was traditionally the easiest way to announce to the world that you were a hard man who had played a lot of rugby in your youth. Regular friction and bashes to the head, usually as a forward participating in the scrum, gradually causes cartilage to deteriorate and cauliflower ears to blossom.

Underwear, skins and catching gloves

• Skins
The lightweight long-sleeved skin is a wonderful invention in the face of the typical rugby climate. Working as a base layer, skins come in varying quality and price and are worth the investment. If there happens to be a two for one offer on, die-hard spectators should consider investing in one for themselves!

• Body armour
At some point your child might have their head turned by the figure enhancing qualities of body armour. Opinion is divided over whether wearing padding in junior rugby is a good idea. If your child has the physique of a twiglet it is tempting to give them some extra padding. However, many feel it prevents children from learning to tackle properly and may actually make collisions more dangerous for those not wearing it.

• Compression or cycling shorts
Worn under rugby shorts and made of lycra, budgie smugglers, sorry, cycling shorts have widely replaced the athletic supporter, otherwise known as the jockstrap. Rugby shorts have traditionally been on the skimpier side and the cycling shorts keep muscles warm and prevent the curse of many a sporting star: chafing.

• Catch gloves
Beloved of the stars of junior rugby teams, these gloves are made of lighweight material to help players catch and grip the ball. Who doesn't want to minimise the handicap of cold, stingy palms on a bitter winter afternoon?

Full-Time

> In this day and age of safety first, of seat belts and cycle helmets, low cholesterol butter, 'Warning: Smoking is a health hazard' - when so much is sanitised and safe - the opportunity to feel that sort of battle-knell thrill comes less and less often. But it is there in rugby, long may it remain"
>
> *Peter Fitzsimons, Australian journalist and Wallaby.*

We hope this book helps you keep pace with the evolving energy and passion of your player on the pitch. This translation of the 15-a-side game should remain clutched in your gloved hand as that tentative child you have been supporting morphs over the years to become a grown-up, glory-seeking warrior.

We would like to thank our rugby-mad husbands and sons for their careful reading and patient explanations. Thank you also, to the school and club rugby teachers who continue to inspire our children. A particular thank you to Charles Welch at Witham Hall School who has supported us so enthusiastically throughout our translations.

The bacon butties are on us!

Appendix

Tag rugby for children

Tag rugby has been developed to strip rugby back to its roots... that is to chase and catch the player with the ball! There is *no* tackling. It's played at mini and junior team level to suck children into loving the essential skills required to play the game and takes away the messiness of tackling or contact rugby. Tag rugby is played until Under 8's, after which different rules apply (see page 91).

• **The rules of Tag rugby**

- The aim of the game is for a team to put the ball down on the ground on or behind the opposing teams try-line. For this, 1 point is awarded.

- It's played with between 3 and 7 players per team.

- Each player wears a velcro belt around their waist and from these, a pair of ribbons or tags hang down on either side of their body.

- Only the child carrying the ball can be tackled.

- Players must always pass to the side or behind, never forward.

- The game begins with a tap and pass and the ball must always be carried in two hands.

- A tackle is made when another player pulls off one of the tags and shouts "tag" while holding it up above their head for the referee to see.

- At this point the ball carrier must stop and pass the ball within 3 seconds or 3 steps.

- If they don't, the ball goes to the opposite team.

After being tagged the player and his tagger are temporarily out of the game as the tag is handed back and reattached.

The side with the ball are known as the attacking team. As they run with and pass the ball they have 6 tags or plays within which to try and score.

When the sixth tag is made then there's a changeover and the attacking team become the defending team and the defending team are given the ball.

There are no scrums or line-outs and no tackling.

"Run at spaces, not faces!"
Translated:
Tag rugbys mantra for teaching children
one of the fundamental skills of the game
- finding space.

Getting children playing

• **The 'New Rules of Play' from England Rugby (Sept 2015)**

The game of rugby and its rules evolve all the time. Just as you get to grips with them, they are bound to change again!

England Rugby, better known as the RFU, introduced a new 'Play and Player Progression pathway' for schools and clubs to follow. Rolled out for the 2015/2016 season, the new programme tweaks the rules of youth rugby to make early experiences of the game more inclusive to all players. Specialising in positions from an early age is stopped and tackling introduced later.

Children play within their age groups. The traditional Colts format, where two age groups play together, has been removed. The new rules apply to children from the U9 age group (where Tag rugby finishes) to the U13 age group. Traditional 15-a-side rugby is played from U14.

Age and school year	Tackle	Scrum	Line-out	Contest for the ball in a ruck and maul	Kicking
U9 7 a-side	Yes - or a 3 sec 'hold' counts as a tackle.	No	No - free pass.	No	No
U10 8 a-side	Yes	Scrum formed by nearest 3 players. Team with the put-in wins the ball.	No - free pass.	Yes - with one supporting player only.	No
U11 9 a-side	Yes	Scrum formed by nearest 3 players but no pushing. Both sides try to hook and win the ball.	No - free pass.	Yes - with two supporting player only.	No
U12 12 a-side	Yes	Scrum formed by nearest 5 players but no pushing. Both sides try to hook and win the ball.	No - free pass.	Yes	No
U13 15 a-side	Yes	Yes - 6 trained players.	No - free pass.	Yes	No
U14 15 a-side	Yes	Yes - 8 trained players.	Yes - but uncontested with only 13 players.	Yes	Yes

It's worth noting that there's no kicking at goal for conversion points until U14, so the traditional sight of rugby goal posts at junior schools could be a thing of the past. Adult rules are introduced at age 15.

Glossary of rugby terms

- **Advantage** - when the referee decides to let play continue despite a minor infringement by one side. He does this when the non-offending team already have the upper hand and when stopping the game would be to their disadvantage.
- **Against the head** - winning the ball at the scrum even though the other team has put it in.
- **All Blacks** - the national team of New Zealand.
- **Back line** - these are the backs waiting fanned out in a line, ready to attack or defend.
- **Backs** - the seven players wearing shirt numbers 9 to 15.
- **Back row** - confusingly, they are the forwards who make up the back row of the scrum.
- **Back three** - they *are* backs - the full-back (no 15) and the two wings (no 11 and 14).
- **Barbarians** - The Barbarian Football Club, affectionately known as the Baabaas, is a UK-based invitational team of internationals and rising stars who play a few matches each year. Players wear a black and white strip with their club teams socks.
- **Binding** - the particular and careful way that a players hold onto other players in the scrum, rucks and mauls.
- **Blind side** - the space on the pitch between the ball and the nearest touchline.
- **Box kick** - a high kick into an imaginary box over the heads of the opposition.
- **Breakdown** - the anarchic scrabbling around when neither side has possession of the ball i.e. the ball is being contested.
- **Cap** - Sometimes an actual cap, presented to players after international games, a huge honour.

Glossary

- **Centres** - the two backs of the inside centre (no 12) and the outside centre (no 13), they stand in the middle of the back line.
- **Channel** - the path through the players legs for the ball to pass out of the scrum.
- **Charge down** - when a player blocks the kick of another.
- **Chip and chase** - also known as a chip-kick pass, a short kick over the head of an opponent in close proximity.
- **Clearance kick** - a distance kick to put the ball into touch and take pressure off the defending side.
- **Conversion** - a kick at goal following a try. If the ball sails successfully over the bar and through the posts 2, points are awarded.
- **Cross kick** - a kick across the field in search of space or another player.
- **Dead-ball** - when the ball is out of play.
- **Dead-ball line** - the last line at each end of the pitch behind the goal posts. If over this, then ball is out of play.
- **Decoy** - a player sent to trick the opposition into believing they are taking the ball.
- **Dive pass** - passing whilst diving towards the receiver, favoured by scrum-halves.
- **Drive** - forwards push ahead by using their legs hard against the ground.
- **Driving/rolling maul** - a maul that moves and pushes the opposition back.
- **Driving tackle** - a tackle that pushes its victim backwards.
- **Drop-goal** - gained by a drop-kick that goes over the bar and through the posts.
- **Drop-kick** - the ball is dropped from the hands to the ground and kicked on the upward bounce.

- **Drop out** (**22 metre**) - a restart by the defending team with a drop-kick from behind their 22 metre line.
- **Dummy pass** - a pretend pass - very satisfying if the other team falls for it.
- **Engagement** - when the 2 front rows of the scrum come together.
- **Extra time** - time added on at the end of the match (at the referee's discretion) for injuries and stoppages.
- **Fast pass** - used by someone who has just caught the ball, only to realise they are about to be tackled!
- **Feed** - the rolling of the ball into the scrum by the scrum-half.
- **Fend off** - also called a hand off, a push with the open hand (NOT to be confused with a punch) used by the player with the ball to shove away an attacking player.
- **Field of play** - the rugby pitch between the two dead-ball lines and touchlines.
- **Flanker** - the two players on either side of the back row of the scrum (blindside no 6 and openside no 7).
- **Flick pass** - a pass, used over short distances with a flick of the wrist.
- **Fly-half** - the back who stands between the scrum-half and the inside centre (no 10).
- **Foot up** - a naughty, illegal move by the hooker in the scrum when he lifts his foot before the ball has been put into the scrum by the scrum-half.
- **Forwards** - the eight players involved in the scrum and wearing shirt numbers 1 to 8, involved in the scrum, line-outs and key to rucks and mauls.
- **Forward charge** - just as it sounds, the terrifying sight (for the players in the way) of a forward with the ball in hand, ploughing through players to make ground.

- **Forward pass** - when a player passes the ball ahead instead of behind and so breaks the key law of rugby. Instantly penalised, although a side pass will be allowed.
- **Foul play** - dangerous actions, against the spirit of the game such as obstructing, stamping and kicking - could result in a yellow or even red card.
- **Fourth official** - positioned on the touchline overseeing substitutions.
- **Free kick** - awarded for minor infringements - can be used to kick to touch, form a scrum or to tap the ball and run.
- **Front five/tight five** - the collective name for the front row (no 1, 2 and 3) and the second row locks (no 4 and 5)
- **Front on tackle** - Please?! As it says.
- **Front row** - of the scrum and made up of the two props (no 1 and 3) and the hooker (no 2).
- **Full-back** - a back and player otherwise known as the last line of defence (no 15).
- **Full-time** - the end of the match.
- **Gain line** - an imaginary line to mark the starting position of the ball in any phase of play. When the attacking team have moved past that line they have gained ground in that phase of play.
- **Gang tackle** - when more than one attacker tackles the player with the ball.
- **Garryowen** - sounds like someone in a boy band, in fact an up and under kick.
- **Gouging of eyes** - dirty tactic used under cover of the scrum, ruck or maul which can result in a red card.
- **Goal-line** - the same as the try-line (see try-line).
- **Goals** - you can not miss them - the 'H' shaped posts at either end of the pitch.
- **Grand slam** - when one team in the Six Nations Championship has beaten all the other 5 teams.

- **Grubber kick** - short kick along the ground.
- **Haka** - the iconic war Maori chant, performed by the New Zealand rugby team to intimidate their opponents before each match. Fiji, Tonga and Samoa also have their own Haka.
- **Half-back** - scrum-half and fly-half.
- **Hand off** - when the ball carrier pushes a potential tackler away with his open hand, also known as a fend off.
- **High ball** - a very high kick which gives players time to rush to catch it.
- **High tackle** - an illegal tackle, not below the shoulders, which can result in a yellow or red card.
- **Hindmost foot** - the back foot of the last player in a scrum, ruck or maul. Players must join a ruck or maul behind this point to avoid being offside.
- **Home nations** - England, Ireland, Wales and Scotland.
- **Hooker** - one of the smallest forwards, he hooks the ball backward in the scrum (no 2) and throws the ball in at line-outs.
- **Hospital pass** - a bad pass, so called because the person who catches it will almost certainly be tackled immediately and need the attention of the doctor.
- **In-goal** - the area between the try-line and the dead-ball line.
- **Infringement** - anything that breaks the laws (i.e. rules) of the game.
- **Inside centre** - the centre closest to the fly-half (no 12).
- **In-touch** - outside the lines on either side of the pitch and so out of play i.e. 'out'.
- **Kick-off** - how all matches are started.
- **Knock-on** - a fumble of the ball where the ball goes forward.

Glossary

- **Line-out** - used to restart a game after the ball has gone into touch (i.e. gone out.) The ball is given to the team not responsible for knocking it out. Their hooker throws it in between the line of tall forwards who jump into the air to try and grab it first.
- **Lob pass** - a pass which travels over the opponents head.
- **Locks** - the two second row forwards (no 4 and 5).
- **Loosehead prop** - the giant on the left hand side of his front row (no 1) supporting the hooker.
- **Mark** - special defensive rule - inside his own 22metre line, a defending player can call "Mark" which is the same as shouting "mine!!". If he then catches the ball he can kick it back up the field and no-one is allowed to stop him.
- **Maul** - a wrestle for the ball between both teams on their feet. A rolling maul is where one team gains momentum and pushes the other side back towards their try-line
- **Mouthguard** - moulded plastic worn in the mouth to protect the teeth.
- **Number 8** - the player at the back of the scrum with no other position name than ...Number 8!
- **Obstruction** - deliberately blocking another player - will be penalised.
- **Offside** - a player is in the wrong place at the wrong time.
- **Open play** - when the ball is being passed freely around the pitch.
- **Openside** - the larger space on the pitch between the ball and the touchline.
- **Out** - over the touchline and off the field of play.
- **Outside centre** - the centre placed furthest away from his own scrum (no 13).
- **Pass** - throwing the ball to a teammate - remember in rugby the ball is never passed forwards.

- **Penalty** - the referee awards a punishment or penalty for a deliberate offence. The non-offending team can then decide to:
  a) tap and go to re-start the game quickly.
  b) take a kick at goal.
  c) kick the ball down the pitch and into touch to get it away and then take a line-out with their own throw-in.
  d) form a scrum with their put-in.

- **Penalty try** - a try is awarded to the attacking team when the referee decides they would have scored a try were it not for foul play by the opposition. The resulting conversion is taken from between the posts - a banker of 2 extra points!

- **Phases of play** - the free flowing parts of the game between breakdowns.

- **Put-in** - what the scrum-half does when he places the ball into the scrum. The team whose scrum-half has the 'put-in' are more likely to win the ball.

- **Punt** - to kick the ball directly from the hand.

- **Red card** - handed out for the worst kind of offences and signals immediate expulsion from the pitch for the player in question.

- **Referee** - he who must be obeyed in all his decisions as he enforces the laws on the pitch. Easily spotted since his kit is still clean.

- **Ripping the ball** - pulling the ball free during a maul.

- **Ruck** - when a player is tackled, falls to the ground and his teammates and the opposition have a pushing contest to get hold of the ball.

- **RFU** - is the governing body for rugby union in England. Also known as 'England Rugby'.

- **Scissor pass** - a switch pass between two players whose runs make an 'x' or open scissor shape.

- **Scrum** - used to restart the game after an infringement - the forwards of the two teams have a pushing contest for the ball.
- **Scrum-half** - the player who puts the ball into the scrum and is the link between the forwards and the backs (no 9).
- **Scrum machine** - a heavy object for the forwards to practice pushing against.
- **Set piece or set play** - a way to restart the match with a scrum or line-out.
- **Side step** - the move that all young players want to perfect - that jig to the side to confuse the defenders before storming on.
- **Sin bin** - the naughty step for players who have been shown the yellow card. Players have to sit out of the game for ten minutes.
- **Six Nations** - the annual competition between England, Ireland, Scotland, Wales, France and Italy.
- **Spear tackle** - a tackle where a player is picked up and dumped down headfirst. Highly dangerous, it's the sort of thing that can land the offending player in the sin bin.
- **Spin pass** - the egg shape of the rugby ball allows it to be spun to travel faster.
- **Super 12 rugby** - a regional tournament played in the southern hemisphere.
- **Support** - one of the key things every player is expected to do for their teammate by carefully following the person with the ball and backing them up.
- **Tackle** - the physical act of bringing the ball carrier down by grasping them below the shoulders and knocking them over.
- **Test** - any game between two international sides.
- **Three quarters** - the centre and the wings.

- **Throw forwards** - this applies to the ball. Should never happen in rugby and is penalised.
- **Tight five** - the front and second row forwards who wrap their arms tightly around each other.
- **Tight forward** - a player from the front or second row.
- **Tighthead prop** - the giant on the right hand side of his front row (no 3) supporting the hooker.
- **Touch judges** - 2 of them support the referee by running up and down the touchline to show where the ball went out (or 'into touch')
- **Try** - the ultimate way to score points in rugby. The ball must be placed on the ground with downward pressure over the try or goal-line. 5 points are awarded and a conversion (kick at goal) is allowed which if successful gains a further 2 points.
- **Try-line** - also known as the goal-line. All players want to get across the oppositions try-line and slam the ball down.
- **Tap tackle/ankle tackle** - last ditch, often-desperate attempt to get the ball carriers legs to collapse.
- **Win against the head** - when the ball is won in the scrum by the team who did not put it in.
- **Wingers** - the backs on either of the left and right wing (no 11 and 14).
- **World Cup** - the highlight of every rugger buggers life every four years.
- **World Rugby** - formerly known as the International Rugby, World Rugby is the world governing body for the sport of rugby union football.
- **Yellow card** - results in the sin bin for ten minutes for very bad behaviour.

Your notes